NORTH AMERICA
THE THIRD LARGEST CONTINENT

Geography Facts Book

Children's Geography & Culture Books

Speedy Publishing LLC

40 E. Main St. #1156

Newark, DE 19711

www.speedypublishing.com

Copyright 2017

North America is the third largest continent on Earth. Let's take a look at all the regions that make up this huge part of our planet.

Broadway
$
$
North America

THE THIRD LARGEST CONTINENT

After Asia and Africa, North America is Earth's largest continent. It touches the Arctic, Atlantic, and Pacific oceans, and connects to South America through Central America. North America is almost 17% of the land area of the Earth, over nine million square miles.

HOME TO MANY PEOPLES

Columbus visited the Caribbean Islands that are often counted as part of North America in 1492, but the whole continent was populated long before the arrival of the Europeans. The first peoples probably crossed a land bridge that existed 15,000 years ago, walking from Siberia to what is now Alaska, and then slowly spreading down to fill both North and South America with varied and complex cultures.

CHRISTOPHER COLUMBUS VISITED
THE CARRIBEAN ISLANDS

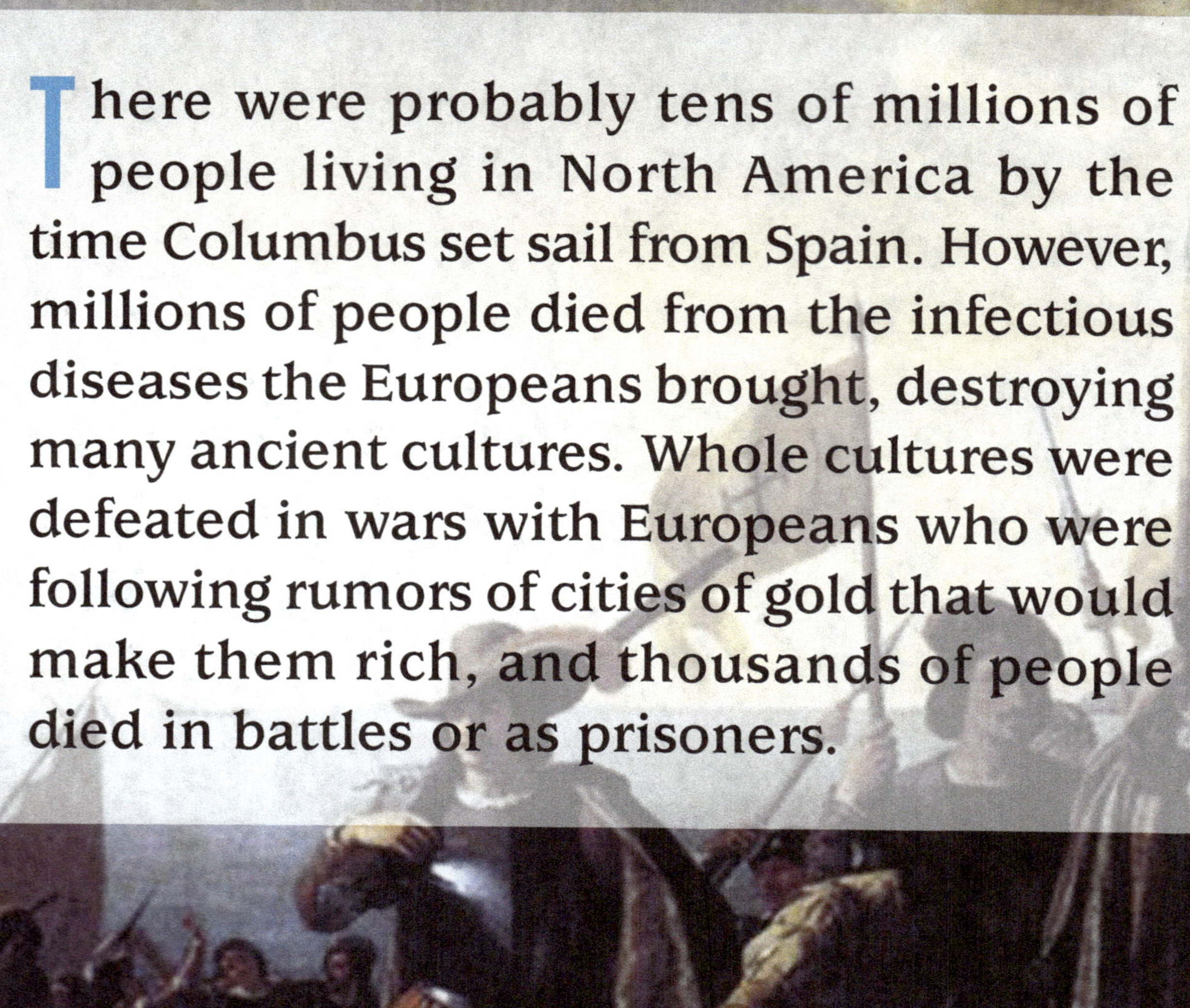

There were probably tens of millions of people living in North America by the time Columbus set sail from Spain. However, millions of people died from the infectious diseases the Europeans brought, destroying many ancient cultures. Whole cultures were defeated in wars with Europeans who were following rumors of cities of gold that would make them rich, and thousands of people died in battles or as prisoners.

In the thousands of years before the Europeans arrived, there were over a thousand different languages spoken by peoples of North America. Now, although the primary languages on the continent are English, Spanish, and French, many native peoples still speak their traditional languages. In the United States, over 200,000 people speak Navajo at home; in Canada, over 100,000 speak Cree.

More than 580 million people now live in North America.

The geological center of each continent is called a craton. This is the most stable and oldest part of the tectonic plate the continent rides on.

The craton that is the center of North America, called Laurentia, is almost 1.5 billion years old.

NORTH AMERICA ON THE GLOBE

CONTINENTAL DRIFT

BEFORE

AFTER

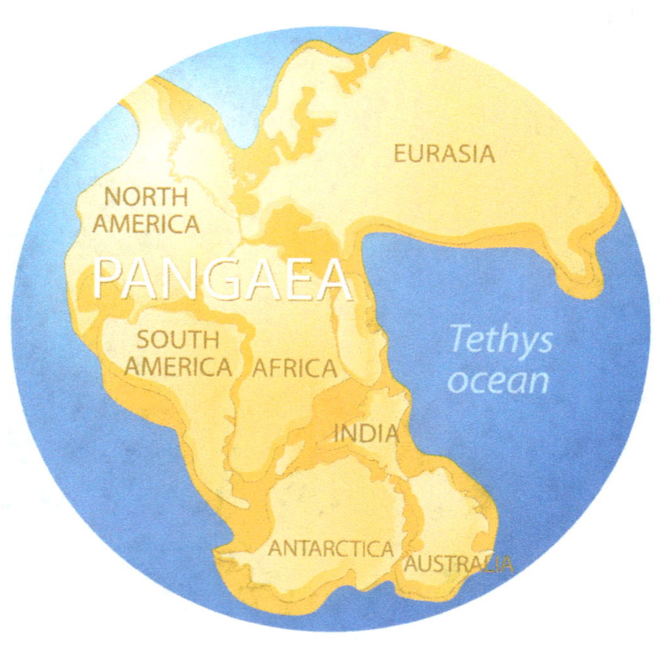

PANGAEA

For millions of years the continents we know now were all part of one super-content, Pangaea. The different elements of Pangaea began to drift apart about 200 million years ago. This drift continues today, although far too slowly for anybody to notice it without scientific instruments.

Central America, joining North and South America, only appeared about three million years ago.

At the other extreme of the time line are the Great Lakes. They formed at the end of the most recent major ice age, as the glaciers that had covered what is now the United States retreated north. The Great Lakes are "only" ten thousand years old.

Pangaea

Laurasia and Gondwana
North America
Eurasia
Africa
South America
India
Tethys ocean
Antarctica
Australia
Modern world
Arctic
North America
Atlantic ocean
Eurasia
South America
Africa
India
Indian ocean
Antarctica

FIVE REGIONS AND MANY BIOMES

Scientists divide North America into five physical regions, and into many biomes. A biome is an area with a fairly stable climate and a stable population of animals and plants. North American biomes include coral reefs, tundra regions, deserts, grasslands, and forests.

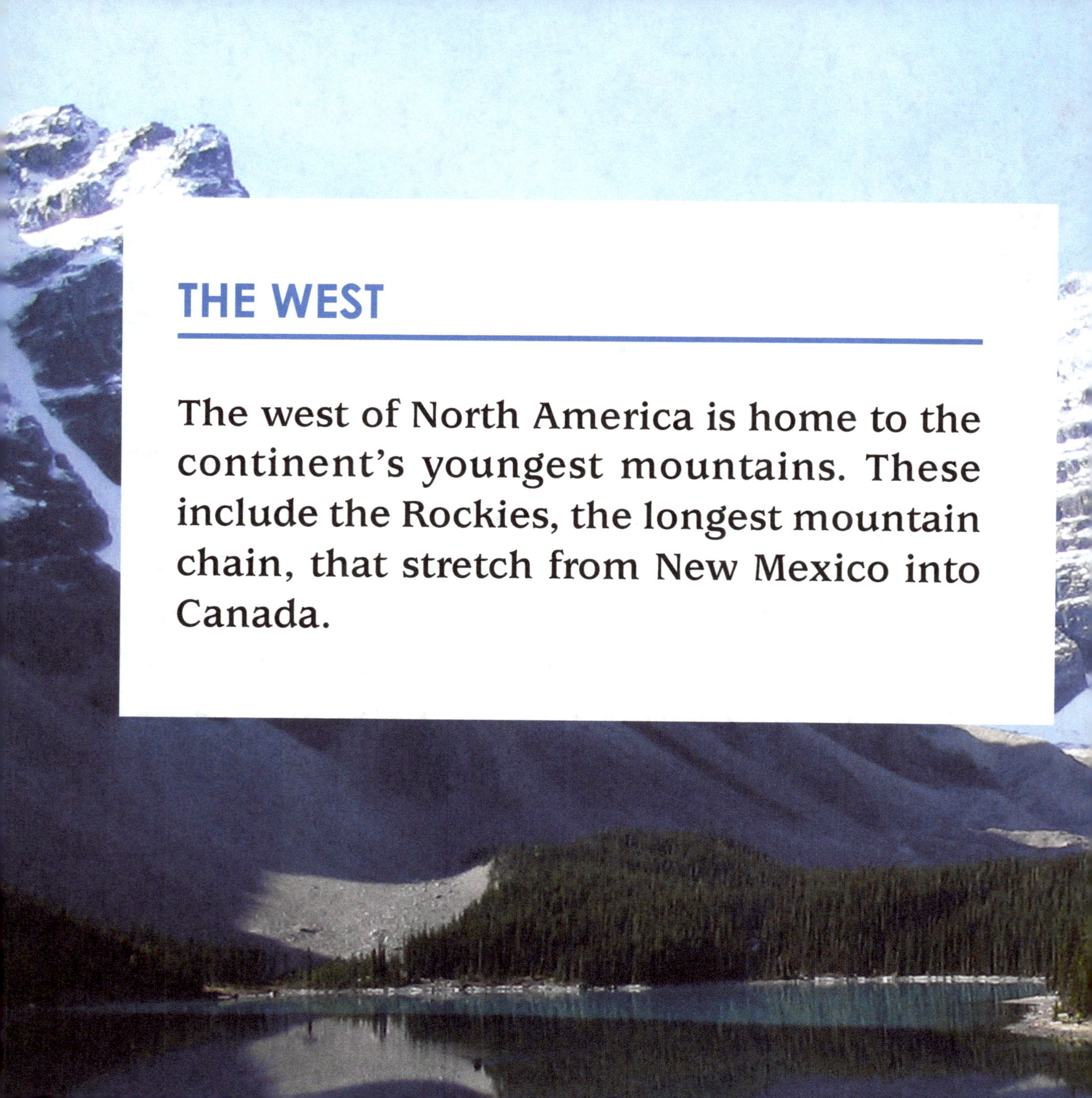

The west of North America is home to the continent's youngest mountains. These include the Rockies, the longest mountain chain, that stretch from New Mexico into Canada.

The Rockies are just one of a series of parallel mountain chains called the Cordilleras. They run from western Canada south as far as Panama, and they have been caused, in part, by the collision of North America's tectonic plate with the tectonic plate under the Pacific Ocean. Where these plates meet, the crust of the earth is rumpled up like a huge blanket

that has been pushed together. Some of these ranges only started to form a million years ago, which is no time at all when you consider how old the Earth is!

Some of the mountains are active or dormant volcanoes. Mount Saint Helen's, in the state of Washington, had a major eruption in 1980. There are ranges of volcanic mountains in the Sierra Madre in Mexico, and in most Central American countries. While eruptions can be destructive, volcanic soil can be rich in nutrients and can create fertile lands years after the eruption has happened.

MOUNT SAINT HELEN'S

RAINFOREST

The western mountains host a temperate rain forest biome, where precipitation is heavy, winters are cold, and summers are mild. There are many species of trees, other plants, and animals that make their home in the temperate rain forest.

The West also hosts North America's major deserts, including the Mojave and the Sonoran. Moist air coming from the Pacific Ocean is blocked by the high western

mountains, so the west coast tends to get most of the rain while to the east of the mountains there is a "rain shadow" of hot, dry wind and deserts.

MOJAVE DESSERT

The deserts are home to cacti of many varieties, and animals like Gila monsters and rattlesnakes. The Baby Professor book Who Lives in the Barren Desert? can tell you more about them.

The northern part of the West has huge deposits of oil and natural gas, much of it in the Arctic or under the Pacific Ocean.

GREAT PLAINS

The Great Plains cover the middle of North America. This area has rich, deep soil that is good for growing. There is also plentiful oil and natural gas under the ground.

KANSAS FARM LAND

The fertile soil came to this area from much farther north, carried south by glaciers about 20,000 years ago. When the Earth grew warmer, the glaciers deposited the rich soil as they retreated north.

The grasslands biome has a wide range of grasses and small bushes, but not a lot of trees. Animals native to the biome include bison, grasshoppers, eagles, and prairie dogs.

AMERICAN BISON

CANADIAN SHIELD

CANADIAN SHIELD

The Canadian Shield is a high plateau that covers much of eastern and central Canada. It is a rocky landscape with an incredible number of lakes of all sizes.

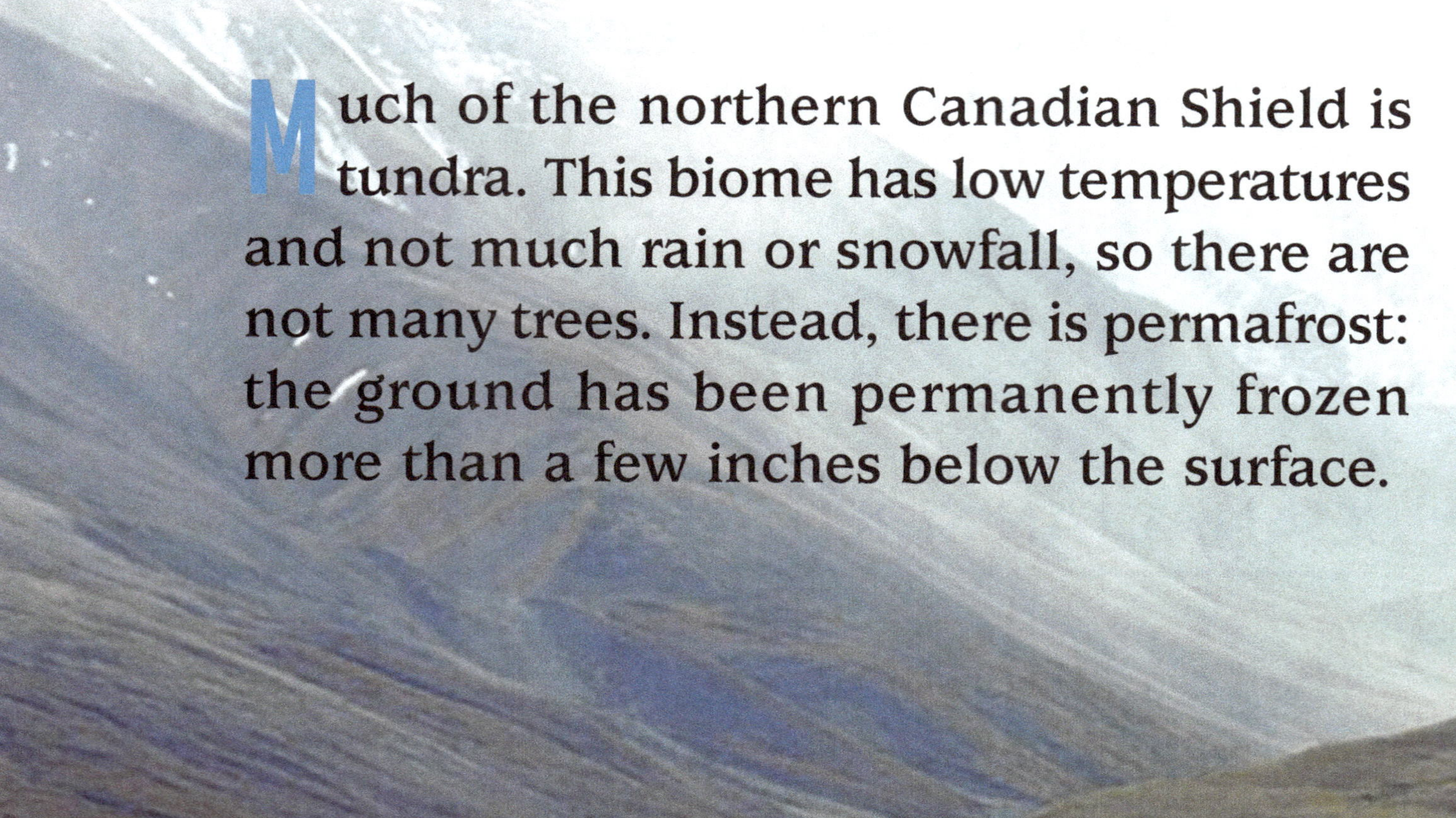

Much of the northern Canadian Shield is tundra. This biome has low temperatures and not much rain or snowfall, so there are not many trees. Instead, there is permafrost: the ground has been permanently frozen more than a few inches below the surface.

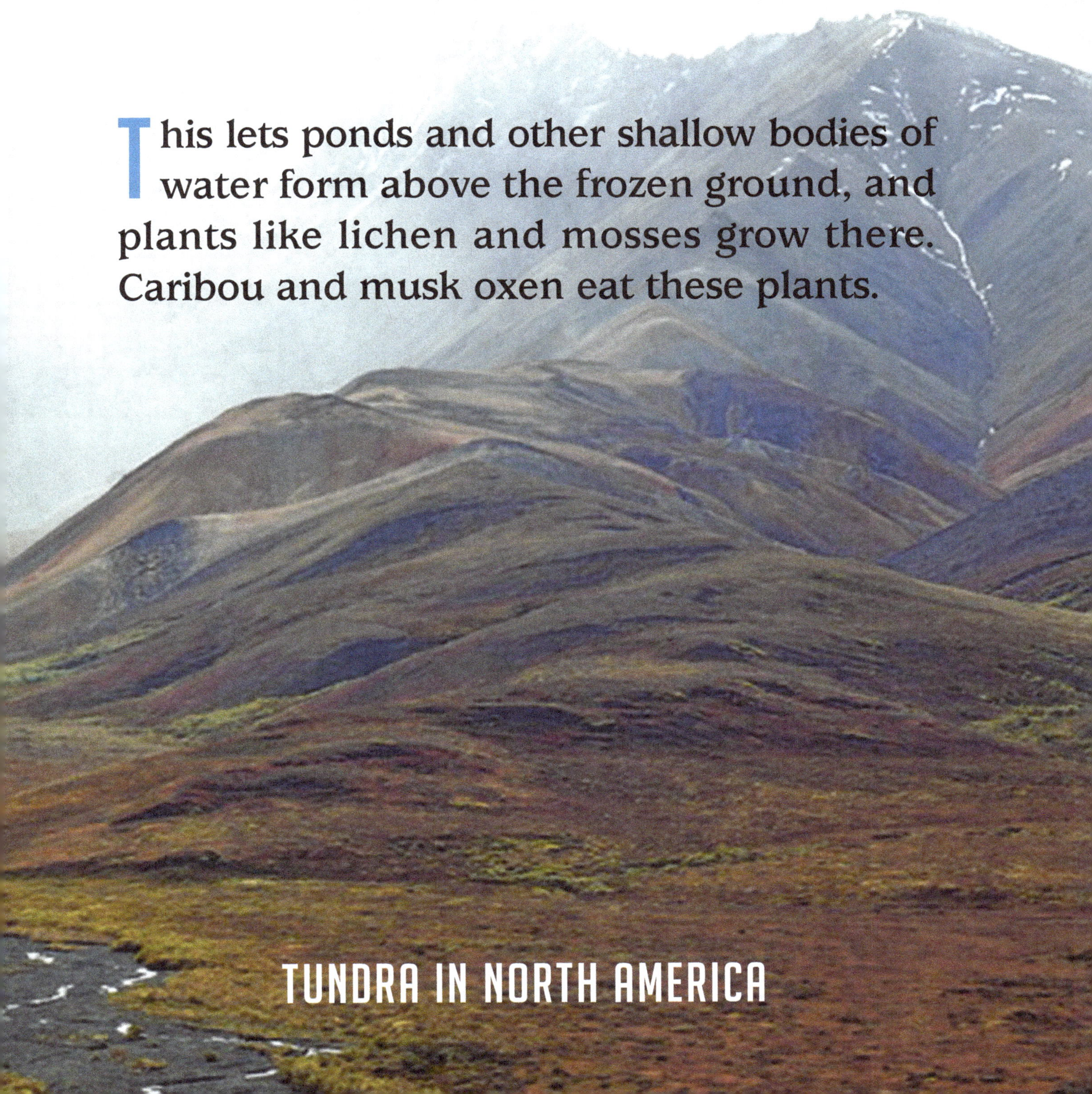

This lets ponds and other shallow bodies of water form above the frozen ground, and plants like lichen and mosses grow there. Caribou and musk oxen eat these plants.

TUNDRA IN NORTH AMERICA

PERMAFROST

Unfortunately, climate change is causing the permafrost to melt in many areas where it has not melted for hundreds of years. In some places this has let the ground collapse into sinkholes. The Baby Professor book *What Every Child Should Know about Climate Change* can tell you more about global warming and its effects on the planet.

EASTERN REGION

The Eastern region includes the Atlantic coast and the older mountain ranges like the Appalachians. The mountains have been mined for coal and other minerals for several hundred years. The coastlands combine river, wetland, and marsh biomes, with plants and wildlife that like a lot of moisture.

FALL IN THE APPALACHIANS

TURNER RIVER, EVERGLADES

Perhaps the wettest area in the region is the Florida Everglades, over four thousand square miles of wetlands. Many plants that flourish in slow-moving water, like sawgrass, make environments for wading birds like herons and ibises.

The Everglades are under threat from pollution, diversion of water to supply growing cities, and spreading towns building into the wetlands.

CARIBBEAN REGION

The Caribbean Region covers more than 7,000 islands, and the waters around them. The Baby Professor Book, The Big Book of Central America and the Caribbean, can tell you more about this region.

CARIBBEAN SEA

DENALI

There is lots to discover about the North American continent. Did you know these fine facts?

Denali, a mountain over 20,000 feet high in Alaska, is the highest place on the continent.

Yellowstone Park has many of the world's most active geysers. This is because the park sits above a huge, ancient volcano. The volcano has not erupted in thousands of years, but it is only dormant, not dead.

YELLOWSTONE NATIONAL PARK WHYOMING, USA

The Bay of Fundy, between New Brunswick and Nova Scotia on Canada's east coast, is long and shallow compared to the open ocean that it is connected to. Its configuration makes more than a thirty-foot difference between high tide and low tide on the Bay.

The Great Lakes hold more liquid fresh water than any other place in the world (Antarctica holds much more fresh water, but it is frozen into glaciers). Lake Superior, with a surface area of almost 32,000 square miles, has a larger surface than any other freshwater body in the world.

The Mississippi River, over 2,300 miles long, is one of the longest rivers in the world.

MISSISSIPPI RIVER VIEW FROM SPACE

There are almost a thousand mammal species native to North America, living in all the many biomes. They range from voles and moles, through rabbits and foxes, all the way up to polar bears and moose.

Death Valley is the hottest and driest place in North America (less than three inches of rain a year), and the furthest below sea level.

DEATH VALLEY

EXPLORE THE WORLD

You are a citizen of Planet Earth: enjoy getting to know your home! Read other Baby Professor books like A Giant Shield, Man vs. Nature: Controlling Forest Fires, and Ocean Tides and Tsunamis to learn even more about our planet.

Visit
BABY PROFESSOR
EDUCATION KIDS
www.BabyProfessorBooks.com
to download Free Baby Professor eBooks and view
our catalog of new and exciting Children's Books

www.ingramcontent.com/pod-product-compliance
Lightning Source LLC
Chambersburg PA
CBHW060225120726
48009CB00003B/147